CW00429080

Beginning Relig

Second Edition

Ray Bruce
Jane Wallbank

Hodder & Stoughton

LONDON SYDNEY AUCKLAND TORONTO

Acknowledgements
The Publishers wish to acknowledge the following who have given permission to use copyright photographs:

The Mansell Collection pp 6t & b, 9t & b, 13, 17, 40 & 66; Janet and Colin Bord pp 10 & 12; The Werner Forman Archive p 14; The Spanish Institute p 15; Barnabys Picture Library pp 18, 19, 21r, 22, 23t, 49, 59, 78 & 79; Museum of Mankind pp 21l, 25, 33, 38 & 46; Hoa-Qui pp 23b, 27, 37, 62 & 84; George A Hall p 24; Harry Price Library, London University p 26; Canadian High Commission p 28; Axel Poignant pp 29 & 89; Australian Information Service pp 30, 31, 56 (M Jenson) & 81 (M Brown); Ronald Sheridan Picture Library p 32; The Horniman Museum pp 35 & 48 (Hamlyn Group); Herbert M Cole p 39; The Victoria and Albert Museum p 41; J Allan Cash pp 42 & 45; Camera Press p 43; The Royal Anthropological Institute pp 44, 47 & 80; Dr Caroline Humphries pp 50 & 52; Redemptorist Publications p 57; The Photo Source p 60; Government of India Tourist Office p 61; Western Americana Picture Library p 63; Camerapix Hutchison Library pp 82, 92 (Peter Montagnon) & 93 (Peter Montagnon); The National Library of Australia p 83; Frank Speed p 85; Zomo Picture Library p 90; George Allen and Unwin (Jean-Louis Nou) p 91.

Drawings by Malcolm Poynter

British Library Cataloguing in Publication Data
Bruce, Ray
    Beginning Religion—2nd ed.
    1. Religion
    I. Title   II. Wallbank, Jane
    200 BL80.2
    ISBN 0 7131 7403 X

First published 1982
Second edition 1985
Sixth impression 1991

Printed in Great Britain for the educational publishing division of Hodder and Stoughton Ltd, Mill Road, Dunton Green, Sevenoaks, Kent, by The Bath Press, Avon.

Contents

1

Everyone Asks Questions . . .

Head-on collision

Since the beginning of human history people have asked questions about themselves and the world around them. Perhaps you can remember asking questions such as:

Where do babies come from?

Why do people have to die?

Where do people go when they die?

Looking at the world of nature you may have asked:

What makes it thunder?

Where does the sun go at night?

Why is it raining?

The questions you asked were all about the things that puzzled you, and the answers you were given may have helped you to understand these mysteries. For example, you may have been told that when it thundered the clouds were banging their heads together! People have always asked questions because they find themselves in a world full of mystery and wonder. The explanations and answers people find as they explore the world form the basis of what they believe.

Things to do

1. Imagine a younger brother or sister has asked you the following questions. What answers would you give that you think he or she would be able to understand? (Perhaps you can remember the answers you were given.)

   What is thunder and lightning?

   Why does it rain?

   Where do people go when they die?

   What is God like?

   Where is heaven?

2. List as many things as you can that are still mysteries for you today.

Everyone believes in something

Our world is a believing world. People have always looked for something in which to believe. Sometimes people have tried to understand the mysteries of life by following a particular religion. A religion centres upon a belief in supernatural powers which control the world in which we live and help explain the meaning of life. Some people call these powers gods and spirits. People believe they can be contacted through worship by, for example, praying and offering sacrifices. In return, they believe, the gods and spirits can help them in their daily lives and in their understanding of the world about them. The Ancient Egyptians and Greeks, for example, believed in many gods who could perhaps be persuaded into giving them whatever they needed.

The Egyptian god Osiris, god of the underworld

The Greek god Apollo riding on his chariot

6

Looking at the world today, we find that people have many different beliefs. Many people believe in the existence of one god. A lot of people read horoscopes in newspapers and magazines, believing that the position of the planets in the sky can have a real effect on the course of their lives. Consider also the power of superstition. Some people believe that omens like a black cat or a horseshoe will bring good luck while walking under a ladder will only bring bad luck. These beliefs actually affect the way people behave. Those who do not believe in the power of any god, spirit or superstition prefer to believe in their own human powers and look to scientists to provide answers to their questions about life.

Things to do

1. Look up the following words in a dictionary and write down the meanings in your notebook: supernatural, horoscope, prediction, superstition and omen.
2. Make two columns in your book, one headed 'Good luck' and the other headed 'Bad luck'. List as many superstitions as you can think of in each column, following the examples given below:

Good Luck   *Bad Luck*
Horseshoe   Walking under a ladder
3. Now divide a page in your book into four sections. In each space draw a picture to illustrate one of your superstitions.
4. Can you think of any other beliefs that people have?

Good luck and bad luck

When did religion start?

Religion is as old as humankind. The earliest evidence we have today concerning the beginning of religious ideas dates as far back as the Stone Age. We cannot be certain as to what Stone Age people believed because they left no written records. We can only guess from the evidence they have left behind. Let us go on a journey back in time to try to discover what Stone Age people believed . . .

Travelling back in time

As we travel back in time to arrive at our destination, it will help us to work out how we number the years. When we want to measure time we must know from where we are starting. You might say, 'What's the problem? We're starting from today'. You might be right. We know what the date is today. But how did we get that date? When did people start counting to make the date what it is, and not some other date?

In the past, people have used many different calendars. Every calendar had a different starting point. Today most people use the same calendar for convenience. This calendar measures time from the year when people thought that Jesus Christ was born. This year is called AD 1. The letters AD are short for 'Anno Domini' and mean 'in the year of the Lord, [Jesus Christ]'. So AD 1 means 'in the year of the Lord, [Jesus Christ], number one'. Man first set foot on the moon in AD 1969.

This is all very well, but what about the years before AD 1? Many people lived before Jesus Christ was born. We date these years by numbering them backwards, beginning from AD 1. The year before AD 1 is 1 BC. (We write AD before a number and BC after a number.) BC means 'Before Christ'.

Non-Christian religions do not use the terms BC or AD, but often say BCE (Before the Common Era) and CE (Common Era). So CE 1 is the same as AD 1. But alongside this they will often have their own calendars which count the years from an important event in their religion. (Find out what starting point Muslims and Jews, for example, use.)

2

The Way Back

We know something about the way in which Stone Age people lived from the science of archaeology. The archaeologist's job is to discover and study the remains that have been left by people who lived long ago. They find, for instance, bones, pottery, tools and weapons. From these discoveries they can build up some sort of picture of how Stone Age people lived and what they believed. Let us take a look at the people of the Stone Age, a period which started over 2 million years ago and lasted until about 2,000 BC.

Archaeologists have discovered flint tools

These carvings have been discovered in the caves and rock shelters inhabited by Stone Age people

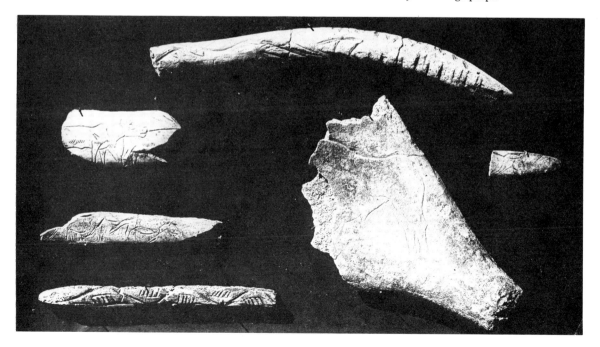

The way of life of Stone Age people was very different from our own. In those days most of the world was covered with forests and the people lived in the open. Stone Age people had to face the dangers of living in a world full of wild animals. They also had to cope with natural disasters such as floods and storms. The main concern of Stone Age people was to survive in very difficult conditions. They did not have the possessions that we have to make our lives more comfortable and safe such as houses, heaters, cars and good clothing. In their world only the strongest survived because they were at the mercy of the forces of nature around them. These forces were so mysterious that they filled Stone Age people with fear and wonder.

Things to do

1. Draw your own picture of a Stone Age family. If possible, look at one or two books in the library to find out what sort of clothes they wore and some of the activities they might be engaged in.
2. Make a list of the forces of nature that Stone Age people would have had to face, e.g. floods, snow, biting cold winds.
3. Describe a frightening or strange experience you have had involving the forces of nature.
4. If you could choose 10 everyday objects to leave behind for an archaeologist of the future to discover, what would you choose? Remember that from these objects the archaeologist will form a picture of life in our times. Write down the names of your objects and say why you have chosen them.

Stonehenge in Wiltshire, a holy place for Stone Age people

Dreaming of a dead friend

The mystery of death

Archaeologists have discovered evidence which shows that Stone Age people were very interested in death and burial. From this evidence we can build up an idea of what Stone Age people might have believed about death. Their religion seems to have been centred upon what were to them great mysteries which filled them with fear and wonder. One of the things that puzzled them, as it puzzles us today, was the mystery of death. Why did people die? What happened to people when they died? We still find it difficult to answer these questions even though we have more knowledge. How would you answer these questions? Let us look at what archaeologists have discovered about Stone Age burial and try to guess what they thought about death.

How Stone Age people buried their dead
Archaeologists have discovered from skeleton remains that Stone Age people buried their dead with great care. The dead bodies were often tied up in the shape of a foetus like an unborn baby in the womb. Some bodies were splashed all over with a kind of red colouring. What possible reasons can they have had for doing this?

It has been suggested that the dead were tied up in the shape of a baby in the mother's womb so that they were ready to be born again into another life. The red colouring represented blood which they knew was important for life. By covering the body with red colouring the dead body was being prepared for this new life.

11

How did Stone Age people come to believe in another life after death? The picture on page 11 might offer one explanation.

Archaeologists have discovered that the dead were buried in shallow graves or caves near to where their friends and relations lived. This may have been done so that contact could be made between the living and the dead. Did the dead people have some special power which the living could use? Were the living friends and relations frightened because they believed that if the dead were not looked after they would haunt the living? It might be for these reasons that the dead bodies were tied up so that they could not haunt anyone. We can be reasonably certain that Stone Age people believed in a life after death since archaeologists have discovered all kinds of flint weapons, ornaments and even food next to the dead bodies. It is quite possible that people of the New Stone Age, about 10,000 BC, even went as far as to bury the wife and servants of a dead chief or king. Why do you think they did this?

Things to do

1. Explain in your own words how the people of the Stone Age buried their dead.
2. Organize a class discussion on the following topic: 'What happens when we die?'

A Stone Age burial chamber in Anglesey

The Mystery of Life

Stone Age people were probably equally puzzled by the mystery of birth — not only of children but also of animals, trees and plants. Stone Age people depended on the birth and growth of different animals so that they would have enough food. What gave life to all these things? It must have seemed that some special power gave life to everything.

Food was needed to prevent starvation and it was necessary that children should be born so that the family or tribe could continue when the older generation died. Therefore the power (or powers) that gave life to children, animals and plants would have seemed very important to them.

Stone Age people showed their concern for these life-giving forces in the sculptures and cave paintings left by their artists.

Female statues
Stone Age people seem to have worshipped a Mother Goddess who represented this life-giving power, the power of fertility. Worship of the mother goddess began in Russia and spread to Europe. Archaeologists have discovered many female figures which Stone Age sculptors created to represent this life-giving power. Why do you think they represented this power in a female form?

In all these figures the thighs, breasts and hips are very large. These parts of the body are important during pregnancy. The figure of the pregnant mother was a symbol of life, not only of human life but of all life, including that of animals and plants. These figures would have been used in ceremonies to make sure the power they represented would produce new life.

A mother goddess, the Venus of Willendorf

Things to do

1. Use a dictionary to find out for yourselves the meaning of the following words: fertility and symbol. Write down these meanings in your notebook.
2. Symbols are all around us today. We find them by the sides of roads and in buildings. Make simple drawings of five symbols and explain what each one represents.
3. Think of your own mother. What does she represent to you?
4. Draw your own picture of a mother goddess.

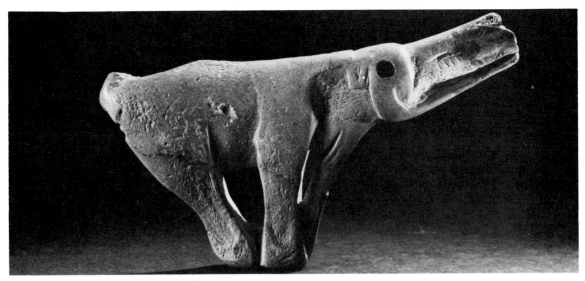

This is a mammoth carved from the antler of a reindeer, which was perhaps the handle of a spear. It was carved by the same people who made the cave paintings—could it have a similar magical purpose?

The search for food

Stone Age people needed a plentiful supply of food—not only food provided by fruit and berries but also meat. Animals had to be found and killed. Bison, bear, deer and horses were important sources of meat. However, they were difficult to catch since they could run faster and were stronger than the hunters. How were Stone Age people to make sure that they would be able to catch enough animals to eat? Perhaps a clue can be found in the strange and mysterious paintings that they drew.

During the last 100 years many exciting and often accidental discoveries of cave paintings have been made, particularly in France and Spain. Two important areas where these paintings have been found are at Altimira in Northern Spain and in the Dordogne valley in France. Most of these cave paintings were done between 25,000 and 10,000 BC.

The cave paintings are something of a mystery because some of them were discovered in the deepest and darkest parts of the caves. Why did the Stone Age artists hide their work? Was it because the cave paintings had some mysterious and secret purpose? Again, we can only guess as to why they were painted in these places.

Most of the pictures are of animals that would have been hunted for food. Some of the animals were painted with arrows and spears in their sides. One explanation for this is that Stone Age people believed that by painting an animal with a spear in its side they would be more likely to be able to catch the animal by some mysterious means. The paintings were done to control the mysterious power which would make sure that the hunt was a success. This is a type of magical belief. By painting a picture of hunting and wounding an animal they believed that this would happen in real life. At the same time, the feeling of being able to catch the animals by painting them would increase the courage and confidence of the hunters. The animals would no longer appear so frightening and fierce.

(*opposite*) A Stone Age cave painting from Spain. What do you think is going on in this picture?

14

The prospect of having fresh meat would have excited Stone Age people. In their excitement they would have danced, sung and cast spells in front of these pictures. It is quite possible that a particular person may have led the dancing in a kind of hunting ceremony.

Some of the paintings show a human figure among the animals who is partly disguised as an animal. He could have represented an animal spirit but was more likely a magician. Stone Age people believed that this magician had the power to control the animals. In their actual ceremonies the magician might have recited some magical spells to help the hunters catch the animals.

Excitement after the hunt

A picture of a 'sorcerer' or magician. Why is it disguised as an animal?

This cave painting is thought to represent a magician or sorcerer. The picture is of a human being wearing some animal disguises. He has a human face and beard, the eyes of an owl, the claws of a lion, the skin and tail of a horse or wolf, and the antlers of a deer. These animal disguises made him feel part of the animal world and he may have felt that such disguises gave him special powers of communication with the animals. Why do you think this magician is wearing all these animal disguises?

The places where the pictures were painted would have been very sacred. The word 'sacred' is very important and to understand its full meaning you should look it up in your dictionary. For the moment here is a simple explanation. If it is used to describe a place or person, then that place or person is very special indeed, completely set apart from what is ordinary. They are special because that person and place is connected with the religious beliefs of people. Can you think of a sacred person we have talked about already?

Things to do

1. Imagine you are a cave painter. Describe why your work is valuable to your people.
2. Draw your own cave painting on poster paper to go on your classroom wall.
3. If you were a cave painter working today, what sort of things would you paint? You must remember that Stone Age artists painted the animals that they wanted for food.
4. Now that you know what the word 'sacred' means, make a list of sacred people and sacred places that you know about.
5. Draw a chart in your books to show the archaeological discoveries we have been looking at in this chapter. You can use the following pattern to help.

Discovery	Where found	What they could mean
Statues of mother goddesses	Russia and Europe	

3

The World of Gods and Spirits

Despite the archaeological evidence, however, we can still only guess as to what Stone Age people believed. But we can say that questions about life, death and survival appear to have led them to some fundamental religious beliefs. Is there any way we can find out more about these fundamental beliefs? Many scholars think we can try.

There are many people today who live in societies that have changed very little over the centuries. We call these groups of people 'tribes' and they live in such places as Africa, Australia, South America and Asia. Scholars think that if we study their religions we might have some idea about the earliest religious beliefs of humankind which will add to what the archaeologists might tell us.

Things to do

1. Use the library to find out about *one* of the following tribes, and write down five sentences describing how they live:
   (a) the Yoruba of Nigeria in Africa;
   (b) the Eskimos of the Arctic;
   (c) the Maoris of New Zealand;
   (d) the Pygmies of the Congo in Africa.
2. Why do you think tribal societies have changed very little over the years?

Most tribal people believe that nothing happens by accident and they picture a world full of magical and supernatural powers that influence the course of their lives. Sometimes these powers are thought of as gods and goddesses who think and act like human beings but have a great deal more power. Sometimes they are thought of as invisible spirits. Tribal people usually attach great importance to these powers no matter whether they are good or evil.

Let us look at some of the ways in which tribal people think of these powers.

Where do you think the people in these two pictures live? What sort of life do you think they lead?

Mana or power

'Mana' is the name used by the people of Melanesia in the Pacific Ocean to describe the power which is found everywhere and which is responsible for everything that happens. These people believe that Mana is all around them even though it is invisible and cannot be touched or seen. In many ways it is rather like our idea of electricity. The Melanesians believe that Mana is there because of what it can do. Some tribes in Uganda, in Africa, have a similar idea of an invisible power but their name for it is 'Jok'. Certain places and objects, such as an oddly shaped stone or a peculiarly shaped tree, are felt to contain more Mana than others and so they are especially sacred. Mana is also present in a natural happening such as a waterfall or spring. It is responsible for the blessings of health, children and good luck. This power can give a person great strength and skill but it can also bring misfortunes such as sickness, death and drought. Just as we treat electricity with great care, so the Melanesians treat Mana with respect. The people want to find this power in their surroundings because of the good it can bring yet, at the same time, they are frightened of it because of the harm it can do.

Things to do

1. Mana is thought to be a power that can help or harm. In what ways is electricity similar?

Power we take for granted

The Spirits

Among tribal people all of nature and life is controlled by many powers called 'spirits'. These spirits do not have bodies but are believed to be very active. The belief in their existence probably arose because nature is made up of many different forces. Tribal people can feel these forces affecting their lives because they live so close to nature. Many people have to struggle against disasters such as drought and famine. Nature seems to keep some sort of balance most of the time: the sun shines without burning or drying up the land; the rain falls without flooding the rivers so that there is sufficient water for plants and animals to survive. Yet at other times life is made very difficult and the food supply is endangered because the sun burns too hot or the rain falls too heavily. How are such disasters explained by tribal people? One answer is that the spirits of the sun and rain are angry with the people and are punishing them.

Spirits are found in rivers, animals and volcanoes. For tribal people, anything that moves or makes a noise contains a spirit of some sort. It is the spirit within each of these things that makes it active. For example, it is the spirit of the volcano that makes it erupt. It is the spirit of the river that makes it flow peacefully when it is pleased, and yet makes the water torrent and rage when the spirit is annoyed.

A wooden mask representing a spirit. When do you think this mask is worn?

An active volcano in the Solomon Islands

Spirits are found in waterfalls, strangely shaped trees and rocks

This belief that the world of nature contains may different spirits is called 'Animism'.

Things to do

1. Look again at the examples you have been given of spirits in nature. Make a list of other natural forces which you think tribal people believe would contain spirits.
2. Explain in your own words why tribal people believe in spirits.
3. Draw the spirit of one of the things mentioned in this section, showing how it behaves when it is pleased and how it behaves when it is angry.

A gargoyle on a church in Wiltshire. Gargoyles were images of evil spirits in Christian art

Other types of spirits
Apart from the spirits that live permanently in, for example, rocks, trees and rivers, there are also spirits which tribal people believe can move about from place to place. These are called 'mobile' spirits. They do not live in any one particular place. They move from place to place, looking after some people and frightening others. Some types of evil spirits live inside human beings and cause great harm.

How tribal people deal with the spirits
We now know that tribal people believe they are surrounded by many spirits, both good and bad. These spirits can affect their way of life by bringing good or bad luck and tribal people believe that trouble comes when the spirits are angry or offended. They believe that all the good things in life come from the good spirits. Sometimes one particular spirit can be both good and bad. It is therefore necessary for people to protect themselves from the bad spirits, and at the same time keep the good spirits on their side.

We shall see in a later chapter how they do this. Perhaps you already have some idea of how tribal people protect themselves from the evil spirits.

Ancestor Spirits

The spirits of dead ancestors continue to exist after death and still play an important part in the lives of the living relatives. These spirits are called 'ancestor spirits'. Here is a story from Nigeria, in Africa, which tells of an ancestor spirit:

> 'There was once a young Nigerian who became very ill and suffered from a severe headache. Doctors could not help this young man. Then, one night, he dreamt that he was visited by his father's spirit demanding the sacrifice of a hen. The young man made the sacrifice, his headache disappeared, and he was soon well again.'

In this story the spirit of the dead ancestor, in this case the father, caused an illness which could only be cured by the living relation, the son, offering a hen to the dead father. Dead ancestors demand to be honoured, respected and, above all, remembered. It is thought to be very dangerous to forget or neglect the ancestor spirits as this can bring all kinds of bad luck and disaster. Remember what happened to the young Nigerian in the story.

A carving of an ancestor spirit

A message from the dead

The spirits of the ancestors are thought to stay near to their living relations so that they can be in close contact with the living. The spirits or ghosts of the ancestors appear to their living relations in dreams (*see* page 11). The living relations speak and listen to their ancestors through a 'medium'. A medium is a person thought to have special powers which help him or her to get in touch with the spirits of the ancestors. Many people, today, go to a medium to try to contact a dead relative. The medium holds what we call a 'séance'.

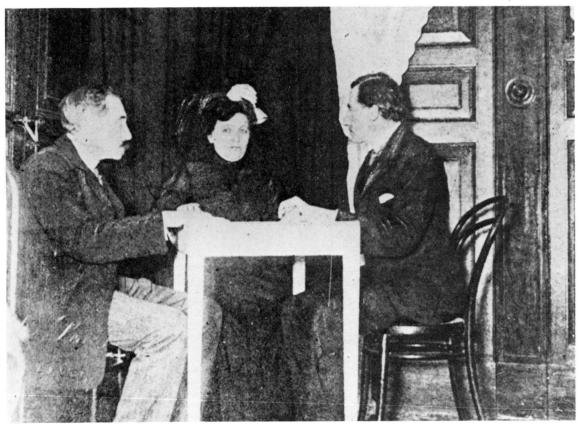

A famous medium, Eusapia Palladino, holding a séance at the end of the last century

How people treat their ancestors

It is very dangerous for many tribal people to neglect their ancestors. They honour and respect their dead by building shrines where they can offer gifts of food, drink and clothing. The living relatives believe that the spirit world is much the same as the normal world and so the dead ancestors need food, drink and clothing.

The ancestor spirits are treated with both affection and fear. They are treated with affection because they were once close relatives and they may have contributed a great deal to the family or

Ancestral shrine. What do you think is going on in this picture?

tribe when they were alive. They are feared because it is thought that they can bring great harm if they are not remembered or not consulted by the living. Especially feared are those ancestors who have been wrongly killed, for it is believed they will seek vengeance on the living. The living relatives have to be very careful how they treat their ancestors because the dead are thought to possess great powers. Offering gifts and prayers is very important if the ancestors are to be persuaded to use these powers to help the living.

Living relations often make symbols and idols to represent the spirits of their dead ancestors.

Things to do

1. Look up for yourself the meaning of the following words: honour, vengeance, shrine, idol. Write down the meanings in your notebook.
2. Write the answers to these questions in your book:
   (a) How are ancestors honoured and remembered by the living in tribal societies?
   (b) Why are ancestors treated with both affection and fear?
3. Write a short story called, 'Ancestor Spirit'. Imagine that someone has a dream in which the spirit of an ancestor appears.

A poem from Africa about ancestors

Those who are dead are never gone,
They are there in the thickening shadow.
The dead are not under the earth,
They are in the tree that rustles,
They are in the wood that groans,
They are in the water that sleeps,
They are in the hut, they are in the crowd.
The dead are not dead.

Those who are dead are never gone,
They are in the breast of the woman
They are in the child who is wailing,
And in the torch that flames.
The dead are not under the earth,
They are in the fire that is dying,
They are in the grasses that weep,
They are in the whispering rocks,
They are in the forest, they are in the house.
The dead are not dead.

Things to do

1. Class discussion. What do you think this poem is saying about ancestors?
2. Write your own poem about ancestors.
3. Copy the picture of the ancestor spirit into your books and then draw a different one of your own.

Totem Spirits

Another type of spirit is the 'totem spirit'. There is a special link between some tribes and a particular animal, plant or bird. The tribe believes that a powerful spirit lives in this creature or plant, and that this spirit works for the good of the tribe. The tribe often takes its name from the animal or plant and this becomes the totem, or emblem, of the tribe. For example, certain North American Indians

(Amerindians) have animals such as the bear, the beaver and the wolf as their totem animal. These animals are highly respected by the tribe and must never be killed except in very special circumstances, such as in preparing for a sacred meal. In this way the people maintain a close link between themselves and the spirits of nature.

An Amerindian totem pole

Things to do

1. Find out as much as you can about the totem spirits honoured by the Indians of North America.
2. Look at the picture of a totem pole. Copy it into your books. Why do you think the North American Indians carve them? Write down your reasons in the form of a caption to your picture.

A special study — Dreamtime of the Australian Aborigines

The Aborigines of Australia believe in a supernatural world called 'Dreamtime'. This is a world of supernatural creatures which exists outside the normal world, but alongside it.

An Aborigine hunter preparing for the kill

The kangaroo, a Dreamtime creature, is thought to have been responsible for helping Aboriginal tribes

In the beginning, the Dreamtime world and the normal world were joined together and the creatures of the Dreamtime wandered over the world creating everything in it. They created all the plants, animals and human beings. They were also responsible for forming the rocks and water holes. The creatures of Dreamtime worked out the rules and regulations by which the tribes live.

These Dreamtime creatures are very powerful and whatever they did at the beginning of time has a spectacular effect on the world as the Aborigines know it. For the Aborigines a rock might appear to be the place where a Dreamtime creature once slept. A water hole might have appeared at the spot where a creature had camped. Parts of its body could be seen in the formation of hills and rocks. The presence of the Dreamtime creatures is felt to be everywhere. Any place connected with the Dreamtime creatures is considered to be very sacred because it is thought that this is where they left their spirits and Aborigines can get in touch with the Dreamtime world at these particular places.

Drawings of Dreamtime creatures found on rock walls in Australia. What do they remind you of?

Each Aboriginal tribe is connected with a Dreamtime creature which was responsible for starting that tribe and looking after it. This creature is the totem of the tribe (*see* previous section) and through the totem, the tribe is in contact with the Dreamtime world. One Aboriginal tribe has a red kangaroo, called 'Koopoo', as its totem animal. The tribe believes that Koopoo led the tribe from one part of Australia to where it lives now (*see* picture).

The Aborigines' way of life, hunting, gathering food, and travelling from place to place, is based on the way it is believed that the Dreamtime creatures lived. The Aborigines follow their example because these creatures are very sacred. When a person dies, the spirit of the Aborigine joins the Dreamtime world.

Things to do

1. Try to find a book in the library that describes the life of the Australian Aborigines. Write down five sentences in your notebook describing the way they live.
2. Why do you think the Aborigines call their spirit world 'Dreamtime'?
3. Copy the pictures of Dreamtime creatures into your book.

31

Gods

Many tribal people picture the supernatural powers at work in the world as gods. The world is controlled by beings that resemble men and women in some ways, but have far greater power. These gods are superhuman and responsible for all that happens in the world. Like humans, they may marry, have children, and fight against each other. There are many sorts of gods and goddesses. Some are powerful creators, others look after the tribe, and others have special jobs to do. Some are good, others are evil. They have to be worshipped as they may affect the life of the tribe in every way.

This belief in the existence of many gods we call 'polytheism'.

Things to do

1. What does the word 'god' mean to you? Write a short explanation in your notebook.
2. Explain what you think is the difference between the gods and spirits.

A sacrifice being offered to the Creator God Nyame worshipped in Ghana

Supreme gods and creator gods

Tribal people may believe in a variety of gods with whom they come into daily contact. Some may also believe in a chief or supreme god who is in control of all the others. In Africa, the supreme god is known by different names among different tribes. Here are some examples.

In East Africa the supreme god is known as 'Osanobwa', which means 'god who carries and protects the universe'. He is also known as 'Chukwu', which means 'the immense overflowing source of everything'. Another name is 'Onyame', which means 'a shining being living beyond the ordinary reach of men'. Ask your teacher to help you understand what these definitions mean.

The supreme god is usually very mysterious and difficult to get to know. As you will see from what the different names mean, the supreme god is seen to be very powerful and is particularly responsible for the creation of all things. The supreme god is distant from them, but is, nevertheless, in all places keeping a close watch on the affairs of men. He is like a great king whose servants and officials are the lesser gods. The supreme god makes his wishes known through the lesser gods. He is rarely approached directly as he is too far away and is so powerful. He is unlikely to get involved in the day-to-day problems of the tribe but he is called upon in moments of great crisis, usually when prayers to the other gods have failed.

Let us look more closely at some of these supreme gods.

Olorun—the supreme god of the Yoruba people of Nigeria
Olorun is god of the sky and is pictured as a great king, whose courtiers and officials are his children, the lesser gods. These lesser gods are the representatives of Olorun and each has a particular job to do on earth. Gods like Shango, the god of thunder, and Ogun, the god of iron, are the descendants of Olorun. Olorun himself is not worshipped directly, but the people can get in touch with him through the lesser gods by offering sacrifices and prayers. In much the same way ordinary people would communicate with a king through his officials. Olorun controls the destiny of every man and woman.

Things to do

1. Why do you think the Yoruba picture their supreme god, Olorun, as a sky god?
2. Look up for yourselves the word 'destiny' and find out what it means. People talk about their destiny in life. What do you think they mean?

An image of Shango, god of thunder

Ngai—the supreme god of the Kikuyu tribe of East Africa

The Kikuyu tribe believe that Ngai is the creator of all things and lives in the sky. He sometimes comes down to visit the earth and, during these trips, he is thought to rest on mountains. He visits the Kikuyu to inspect their behaviour and brings with him either blessings or punishments. He cannot be seen by men but his approach is announced by the crash of thunder and the flash of lightning. Normally he takes little interest in the daily lives of the people

The approach of a god is announced by the crash of thunder and the flash of lightning

since he lives so far away. But at important times in the lives of the Kikuyu people like birth, marriage and death (*see* chapter 6) they call upon Ngai for blessings. In their everyday lives the Kikuyu offer no special prayers or sacrifices to Ngai since they take it for granted that if all is going well, then the god is pleased with them. It would be wrong to bother Ngai when all is well. The Kikuyu only call upon Ngai when there is real need, when there is danger, or when they need special guidance.

The Great Spirit—the supreme god of the Lenape Indians of North America

Most of the North American Indians believe in an all powerful and invisible god. Different tribes call him by different names, such as 'the Master of Life', 'Father of the Sky', and 'the Great Mystery'.

The Lenape call him 'the Great Spirit' and he is the leader of all the gods. The other gods are simply his agents or messengers. The Great Spirit is believed to be the creator of the earth and everything in it. He has given the Indians all they have. The people only pray to the Great Spirit during their most important ceremonies when they thank him for all he has done for them. Their daily worship is addressed to the lesser gods, his agents, who are in charge of the forces of nature. The people feel closer to the lesser gods because what they do can be seen in the world of nature; the sunrise, the thunderstorm, the wind. The Great Spirit lives far away in the highest heaven but he continually watches over his people.

Things to do

1. Make a list of the similarities between the three gods described above.
2. Why do you think tribal people believe in a supreme or chief god?

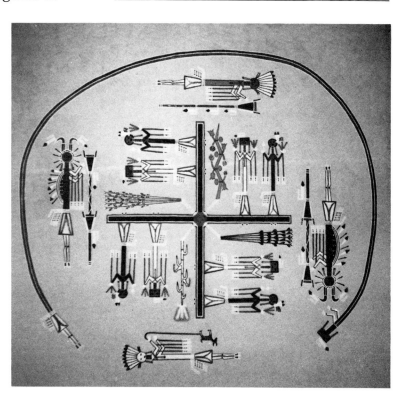

A sand painting made by the Navajos - an Amerindian tribe. It is made to ask the help of supernatural powers in times of bad luck. It shows the gods of morning and of twilight, as well as maize, cotton, melons and tobacco which were brought to the Indians by the gods. The Rainbow Goddess circles the earth. The painting is incomplete - if finished it must be destroyed

The lesser gods

The lesser gods are not nearly so powerful or terrifying as the supreme gods although, of course, they are more powerful than humans. Unlike the supreme gods, they can be flattered, persuaded and even threatened. One African prayer says:

> 'You are useless, you gods. You give us only trouble. You are a bunch of so-and-so's. What do we get from you? Nothing.'

It is clear from this prayer that the people feel that they can have relationships with the lesser gods in much the same way as with human beings.

Each of the lesser gods is thought to control a particular area of human life or have a special job to do. There are gods of the sky, earth, water and forest. There are gods of farmers, fishermen, mothers and hunters. They are regularly called upon depending on the needs of the tribe. For example, if there has been a

Why is this man angry?

drought the people will call upon the water or rain god. At what times do you think members of a tribe will call upon the god of hunting or the mother goddess?

There are many gods and goddesses and they can be good or evil. They are worshipped because they explain the mysteries of life, as do the nature gods whose activities explain the changes in the weather and the seasons. They can be persuaded or bribed to work for the good of the people by the offering of prayers and sacrifices.

As we have seen, many of the gods worshipped by tribal people are closely related to nature. The gods are also related to the sorts of lives that the people lead. For example, where the people are farmers their gods are gods of planting and harvest. Where the people are food gatherers and hunters, like the Pygmies of Africa, their gods are gods of animals and hunting.

Let us look at some of these gods and goddesses.

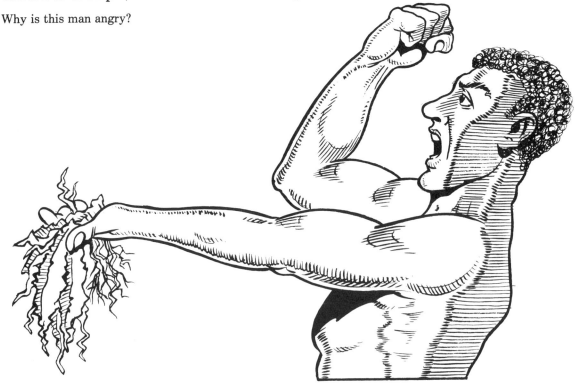

36

A blacksmith in Nigeria making a lucky charm

Ogun—the god of iron

Any member of the Yoruba tribe of West Africa who works with iron would worship Ogun, the god who is believed to have brought iron to the Yoruba. The worshippers of Ogun respect all things made of iron and treat them with special care for it is he who has given them the gift to work with this metal. Workers in iron may keep their tools and weapons in a special shrine belonging to Ogun. Because harvesting tools are made of iron, Ogun is especially honoured at the annual harvest festival.

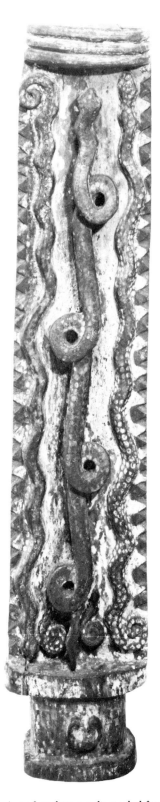

The python god of West Africa

In Africa the python has been one of the enemies of man, taking people by surprise and killing many. People in Africa noticed that once a python had caught and eaten its prey it was far less dangerous; so the practice of making offerings to the python grew up. In the past, humans have been sacrificed to the dreaded snakes. Less than a hundred years ago travellers in Africa saw the python being looked after, fed, watered, and even danced to. The python god was given many wives who brought food and water to him and decorated his house. It was thought that the python god would look after the fortunes of the tribe and warn them of approaching disaster. The penalty for killing a python was death.

Ala—the earth mother of the Ibo of West Africa

The Ibos of Africa worship Ala as the earth mother or earth spirit and she is very popular because she is connected with the earth and nature. Temples contain life-size images of Ala holding a baby in her arms and sacrifices are offered to her to promote fertility (*see* page 13). On special occasions new houses are built for her, and each contains images of various creatures made from clay and painted in bright colours. Ala also watches over the behaviour of the tribe and she is responsible for its rules. She is also the guardian of the dead, who are believed to return to her womb when they are buried in the earth.

A wooden carving of snakes, a cult symbol from Nigeria

Ala, the mother goddess with her children. Where have you seen a picture of another mother goddess in this book?

Sacred pyramids built in honour of Ala

Garelamaisama—a goddess of the Chenchus of India
Garelamaisama is goddess of the hunt and watches over the collection of edible plants. She is thought to have power over the wild animals of the forests and therefore brings good luck to the hunters. These hunters say prayers to the goddess before leaving home to ask for a successful hunt, and if they manage to catch an animal they offer part of the meat to the goddess with prayers of thanks. The Chenchus believe that long ago only male animals were killed because Garelamaisama became very angry if a female was killed. Even now, if a hunter should kill a female animal he prays to the goddess for forgiveness just in case she gets angry. Garelamaisama is believed to have great influence over human behaviour and can, for example, prevent people from quarrelling.

Things to do

1. Make a chart in your book listing the gods you have studied and why they are worshipped. You can use the following plan.

God	Tribe	Why it is worshipped
Garelamaisama	The Chenchus of India	For good hunting

2. Try to find out about other gods of the Yoruba and Ibo tribes of West Africa. Look in the library to see if there are any books on the subject.
3. In your books write an answer to the question, 'Why do people worship different kinds of gods and spirits?'
4. Make a class wall chart called 'The World of Gods and Spirits'. Draw pictures of what you think the gods and spirits, which are mentioned in this chapter, look like.

A hunting scene from the Chenchus of India. Who is doing the hunting?

4

Contacting the Gods and Spirits

We have seen that many tribal people in the world today believe that they are surrounded by powers ranging from Mana to spirits and gods. These powers can do them both good and harm. To make certain that everything good comes to the tribe, the favour of the gods and spirits has to be gained. But how is this to be done? How can the influence of the gods and spirits be gained so that no harm can come to the people? Questions like these can only be answered if contact or communication is made with the gods and spirits.

As you might imagine, not everyone has the special skills and knowledge to make contact with the spirits and gods. In tribal societies it is the job of a 'specialist' person, someone who has the skills and knowledge to make this contact. Perhaps you can think of 'specialists' in our society that you have come across. Probably the best example is the doctor who has the special skill and knowledge to make you better when you are ill. Can you think of any others? What do you think makes a person a specialist?

In tribal societies the person who contacts the spirits and gods is a specialist because he or she might be the only member of the tribe who understands the secret ways of the spirits and gods. This person is the link between the everyday world of men and the supernatural world. Such a person is believed to be sacred. Why do you think such a person is sacred? (Look again at

A Zulu witch doctor

page 17.) Another name for the specialist is the 'holy man'. Find out for yourself what the word 'holy' means.

The holy man often lives apart from the rest of the tribe. This shows that he is somehow different from them. His special skill and knowledge makes him feared and respected by the rest of the tribe. Why do you think the holy man is both feared and respected?

A more familiar name for the holy man is a 'witch doctor'. In Africa, the witch doctor performs all kinds of songs and dances to help the people when they are in trouble and need help. He dresses in bright colours and wears a mask or paints his face. He uses all sorts of 'magical' charms and spells to cure people when they are sick.

The use of 'magic'

The use of magic is a very important part of the holy man's job. Magic means a great deal more to tribal people than performing conjuring tricks with rabbits and cards. Magic is the belief that special words and actions can give a person the power that belongs to a spirit or god. With this power the holy man can bring about both good and evil and can therefore affect the fortunes of the tribe.

If the magical power is put to good use it can be of great benefit to the tribe. Magical charms are used to ward off sickness and evil. Magical mixtures or potions are taken to make people fall in love or ensure that a woman will have a

There's magic and magic

A magician and rainmaker of the Kgatla tribe

baby. These mixtures contain all sorts of ingredients like bird feathers, teeth, dried insects and a variety of dead animals. The Eskimos, for example, use magic to make sure there is a plentiful supply of animals to eat. The Indians of North America use magic in their Corn Dance to ensure that their maize will grow. Can you remember how magic was used by the cave painters? (*See* page 16.)

Magic is also used for evil purposes. A holy man can try to control the power of the spirits and gods for his own selfish purposes, usually with the aim of hurting someone. By using magic in this way, a holy man can put a curse on a person so that his crops or hunting might fail. This magic can make a person ill and even bring about a person's death. The holy man might make a small model of the victim and stick pins into it. As a consequence the victim is expected to feel the pain and perhaps even eventually die. The holy man might

obtain the hair and fingernail cuttings of the victim and then bury them. As these decay in the ground so the victim is meant to die a slow death. There are many stories of people dying at the hand of an evil holy man.

Things to do

1. Can you think of any reason why evil magic might work?
2. In your books write out what you think the difference is between 'good magic' and 'evil magic'.
3. 'Voodoo' is a form of magic practised in some Caribbean islands (especially in Haiti). Use an encyclopedia to find out more about Voodoo and write a few sentences about it in your notebook.
4. Find a picture of a witch doctor and copy it into your books.

A witchcraft stall in Africa. What is being sold and what do you think they are used for?

Two water spirit masks from Nigeria

The holy man at work

The holy man of a tribe has many different jobs to do for the people and he is given a special name for each job that he does. We shall look at these jobs in more detail.

The healer
Probably the most important job of the holy man is that of a 'healer'. Among tribal people sickness and disease is thought to be due to the presence of an evil spirit. A person becomes 'possessed' by an evil spirit and this can make him appear quite mad. Among the tribes of Uganda, in Africa, sickness is believed to be caused by the ghost of a dead ancestor who haunts the living person. Remember the story on page 25. If the person is to be made better then the spirit has to be driven away by the healer. The healer uses his magical spells and potions. He tells the person to wear a lucky charm to keep away the evil spirit. Some tribes believe in the magical properties of water, and a healer will bathe a patient to cure him. The healer uses his special knowledge of plants and herbs to make medicine to cure the person. Some healers use 'quinine' and 'morphine', which are widely used in medicine today.

Things to do

1. Why are quinine and morphine used by doctors today? What effects do each of them have on patients?
2. Write a story which begins, 'The evil spirit had caused a great deal of sickness and death in the village.'

46

The diviner or seer

Another job that a holy man does is that of a 'diviner' or 'seer'. Both these words mean that he can find out secrets or 'see' into the supernatural world of the spirits and gods and discover information that can help the people. The holy man is taken over ('possessed') by the power of the spirit or god and goes into a 'trance' or has a 'vision'. Then the spirit or god reveals a message or relays information and the holy man acts as a medium (*see* page 26).

Things to do

1. Look up the following words in a dictionary and write down their meanings in your notebook: trance and vision.

A mask worn by a tribesman in Zambia

Among the Yoruba tribes of Nigeria, in Africa, the diviner is known as the 'father of secrets'. Why do you think he is given this name?

The Yoruba god of divination is called Ifa, and the diviners who worship Ifa get information from him. The diviners make contact with him when important decisions have to be made, such as who should be made king or when is the right time to go to war.

Another important job of the diviner is to try to discover what will happen in the future. Sometimes this is done by the spirits and gods giving the required information in a vision or dream. On other occasions the diviner uses his special knowledge of nature to read certain signs or omens that will tell him what is going to happen. The flights of birds or changes in the weather are signs which the diviner can read which help

An African Ouija board

him to decide what will happen.

Another way of finding out what the future holds is to study the insides of an animal or bird which has been sacrificed. If a diviner merely wants a simple 'yes' or 'no' answer to a particular question he kills a chicken and is able to tell the answer by looking at the position in which it falls when dead. For instance, if it lies on its back the answer may be 'yes'; if it lies on its stomach the answer will be 'no'. A diviner also throws sticks, stones or bones, and the message he will be able to read will depend on the pattern they make when they fall.

(*above*) What does the future hold?
(*left*) Fortune tellers

Things to do

1. Why do you think the people of the tribe want to know what the future holds?
2. Many people who live in the country read the signs of nature. What do these people think will happen when they see the following signs:
   (a) cows sitting down in a field;
   (b) flocks of birds flying south;
   (c) red sky at night?
   Write the answers in your notebooks.
3. Many people today use certain aids to help them see into the future. Try to think of four examples of aids that you may have heard of. The picture will give you some clues. Now make a drawing of the things you have thought of and underneath write down how you imagine these aids might be used.

49

A special study—the 'shaman'

Many of the jobs we have been looking at are performed by a 'shaman'. The name 'shaman' originally comes from Siberia and the Arctic region, and means 'priest-doctor'. Today the word 'shaman' is often applied to any holy man or woman who has studied the secrets and mysteries of the supernatural world and who has learnt the skills and knowledge that will give them their power. We begin our study by asking the question, 'How does a person become a shaman?'

A person may become a shaman because they feel that is what they want to be. Or it may be because their father was one or because the tribe has chosen them.

A Shaman with his drum standing among the people whom he helps. What does he use his drum for?

Holy man has a vision which only he can see

But probably the main reason why a person becomes a shaman is because they have been chosen by a member of the spirit world. This spirit becomes the shaman's 'spirit help'. Here are two examples showing how a person becomes a shaman.

'Once I (the shaman) was asleep on my sick bed, when a spirit approached me. It was a very beautiful lady. She said, "I am the spirit of your ancestors, the shamans. I taught them how to be shamans. Now I am going to teach you. The old shamans have died, and there is no one to heal the people. You are to become a shaman." I felt very frightened and tried to resist her. Then she said, "If you will not obey me, so much the worse for you; I shall kill you." '

'My body was quivering and I began to sing. A chant was coming out of me without my being able to do anything to stop it. Many strange things appeared to me. I saw huge birds and animals. These were seen only by me, not by others in the house. Such visions happen when a man is about to become a shaman. The songs force themselves out without any attempt to compose them.'

After reading these stories can you pick out the experiences that changed someone into a shaman? To become a shaman involves special training which can bring with it great suffering and hardship. The examples above show this.

51

A shaman is chosen by a spirit and this spirit gives the shaman their power. The shaman uses the songs given to them to call their spirit help. The spirit appears in many different forms:

'. . . sometimes my spirit help looks like a woman, and sometimes she takes the form of a wolf. She is terrible to look at. Sometimes she comes as a winged tiger. I mount it and she takes me to different countries.'

The spirit help is able to control the shaman and as a result they have very strange experiences. The shaman becomes very excited and experiences a state of 'ecstasy'. During these states they can leave their body and travel to parts of the spirit world to discover secrets and gather information. The shaman dances, plays a drum and sings songs. This helps them to be taken over by their spirit help. In this story the shaman goes on a journey to the spirit world to find a lost soul which has made a member of the tribe very ill.

'The shaman sits on the ground and, after drumming for a long time, calls his spirit help. The spirit speaks through the shaman and explains that the soul of the patient has travelled along the road to the Kingdom of the Shadows. The shaman drops his drum and lies without moving. This means that the shaman has left his body and has started his journey to the spirit world. After a while the shaman wakes from his journey and he replaces the soul in the patient's body. He then goes to the door and waves goodbye to his spirit help.'

A shaman drumming for his spirit help to cure an ill member of the tribe

Shamans use their special powers to travel to the spirit world. There they are able to discover secrets that will benefit the tribe, such as the causes of illnesses and diseases. They carry the prayers and sacrifices of the people to heaven and escort the souls of the dead to the same place.

Things to do

1. Now you have read all about the shaman, write a story called, 'The Work of the Shaman' using the information you have been given.
2. Copy one of the pictures of the shaman into your book.
3. Find out for yourselves what a state of 'ecstasy' means. Can you think of any occasion when you have felt 'ecstatic'?

Ways of contacting the spirits and gods

Some of you are probably familiar with the 'Lord's Prayer'. Write out this prayer into your book. (If you do not know it ask your teacher to show you where to find it.) What do you think Christians are asking for when they say this prayer?

The most common way of contacting the spirits and gods is through prayer and it is an important part of worship in all religions. Among tribal people prayers are used a great deal as a way of talking to the gods and spirits. They are spoken by individuals or by the holy man who prays on behalf of the tribe. The main reason that people pray is because they feel dependent on the good will of the spirits and gods and, therefore, people need to get in touch with them. Here are some other reasons why people pray:

(1) to ask the spirits and gods for particular things;
(2) to say 'thank you' for something the spirits and gods have done or given;
(3) to ask forgiveness when a person has done something wrong or has offended the spirits and gods in some way;
(4) to praise the spirits and gods for the interest they have taken in the tribe.
Try to think of different occasions on which prayers are said. Write down the reasons why people say prayers at these times.

Let us look at some examples of prayers. The first example is part of a prayer spoken by the chief of the Blackfoot Indian tribe of North America. This prayer is spoken during the festival of the Sun Dance.

'Great Sun Power
I am praying for my people.
Many are sick and in want.
Pity them and let them survive.
Grant that they may live long and have abundance.
May we go through these ceremonies correctly,
As you taught our forefathers to do.
If we make mistakes, pity us.
Help us, Mother Earth, for we depend on your goodness.
Let there be rain to water the prairies,
That the grass may grow long and the berries be abundant.
Great Spirit, bless our children, friends and visitors through a happy life.
May our trails be straight and level before us.
Let us live to be old.
We are all your children, and ask these things with good hearts.'

What is the chief asking from the 'Great Sun Power'? Why is he also praying to 'Mother Earth' (*see* page 13)? From this prayer can you discover what sort of problems are facing the Indians?

Blackfoot Indian chief prays

Read the following prayers used by the pygmies of Central Africa.

(1) 'Oh God give us mercy upon our children who are suffering.
Bring riches today as the sun shines.
Bring all fortunes to me today.'
(2) 'Grandfather, Great Father, let matters go well with me,
For I am going into the forest.'
(3) 'I thank you for the meat, which you give me.
Today you have stood by me.'

At what times do you think these prayers are said? Which god or spirit do you think the pygmies are praying to in each of the prayers?

Hymns and chants

When people worship they may use hymns and chants to contact the spirits and gods. Hymns and chants are religious songs which are sung or recited by the people. They are often performed by groups of people and are accompanied by music and dancing. Many of you will probably be familiar with hymns but you may be unaccustomed to chants. A chant is a song with a set rhythm and the parts of the chant are repeated over and over again. A good example of a chant that can be heard today is one that you might hear at a football match.

Australian Aborigines taking part in a traditional dance - the Corroboree

The Aborigines of Australia chant and sing a great deal during their religious ceremonies. The people gather together and a leader, called a 'Song Man', starts everybody singing. This man is much respected by the people because he knows all the songs and chants. The songs are accompanied by the noise of boomerangs and sticks which are beaten together. Here is a song that the Aborigines would sing:

'Day breaks: the first rays of the rising sun stretching her arms
Daylight breaking, as the Sun rises to her feet.
Sun rising, scattering the darkness;
Lighting up the land.
With disc shining, bringing daylight,
As the birds whistle and call.
People are moving about, talking, feeling the warmth.
Burning through the gorge, she rises,
Walking westwards,
Wearing her waistband of human hair.
She shines on the sprawling roots,
Its shady branches spreading.'

Things to do

1. Write down two reasons why you think people want to sing hymns.
2. The Aboriginal song is very similar to a hymn that you might have sung. It is called, 'Morning Has Broken'. Try to find the words to this hymn and compare it with the Aboriginal song.

Sacrifice

Among tribal people, the giving of a 'sacrifice' or 'offering' is an important way of keeping the spirits and gods happy. The people believe that by giving something, often quite valuable, the gods and spirits will give something in return. Can you think of reasons why people give sacrifices and offerings to the gods and spirits? (To help you, look back to the reasons why people pray.)

In tribal societies all sorts of things are sacrificed to the spirits and gods. Simple things are offered like water (which is very rare in hot countries), shells, beans, and flowers. Sometimes an animal is sacrificed. The animal is killed and the blood is poured out on an altar,

This photograph shows a Christian priest lifting a cup of wine, which is symbolic of the sacrifice Jesus made on the cross

the place of sacrifice, or left to soak into the ground. The meat is then cooked and shared out among the people. The blood, which represents the life of the animal, becomes the god's share. By offering the blood to the god and eating the meat themselves, they are sharing a meal with the god. Some people burn the animal so that the sweet smell of the meat ascends to the god in the smoke. If you have smelt roasting meat you can understand why the people believe the god will be pleased with this.

In Africa the most common form of sacrifice is a cockerel. More expensive animals, such as sheep or bulls, are offered in times of emergency such as during a drought.

Things to do

1. Think of other occasions when a sacrifice might be made to the spirits and gods. Make a list of them in your notebook.
2. What sort of person do you think would offer the sacrifice?
3. Find a picture of an altar and copy it into your book.

Perhaps the most valuable gift that can be offered is a human being. Although this does not happen nowadays, human beings have been sacrificed in the past. Human sacrifices were normally offered in times of real emergency. In Africa human beings were sacrificed to help a chief or king on his journey to the underworld. Others were sacrificed on the anniversaries of his death so that he might be given news of the living.

In this picture a shaman, on the ground banging his drum, (*bottom left*) is offering a sacrifice to the Supreme Spirit (*top right*) to help a sick member of the tribe (*bottom right*). However, an evil spirit, Kala (*above the Shaman*) is trying to stop the sacrifice. Kala is surrounded by mischievous spirits. In your own words make up a story describing, in detail, what is going on in the picture

58

Holy Places

When we think of a holy or sacred place connected with religion, we think of a special building like a church or mosque. However, tribal people rarely have buildings like ours. Some tribal people build simple temples where a spirit or god is worshipped and where the people offer prayers and sacrifices. A holy man would be in charge of the worship at the temple. In the temple there is a sanctuary or shrine where it is believed the spirit or god is present.

Holy places. (a) A church in England

(b) The Sacred Mosque in Mecca

A temple is one type of holy place but there are many others. For tribal people, almost any place can become holy. It can be a rock, a tree, a cave, the site of a spring or a mountain. The shrine which is built at these places can be simply a pile of stones, a mud pillar or even a piece of wood.

A place becomes holy because it is somehow linked with the supernatural world. A particular spirit or god has revealed its power to the tribe at this place and consequently it has become holy. Or perhaps people have had strange visions there or something like a 'miracle' has happened at that place. For whatever reason, these holy places are very important to the people. They are the places where people go to contact the

(c) A temple by the sea shore in India. What religions are represented in these three pictures?

spirits or gods, to ask advice from them and to find out what they want. The holy place is the centre of tribal life — for if the tribe is to survive then it is important to keep in contact with the gods and spirits. For example, when the Sioux Indians of North America moved from one camp to another, the first thing they built was a new holy place. This became the new centre of their lives because it is the home of the Great Spirit whom they worship.

A tribal temple in Africa

Things to do

1. Explain why you think the holy place is important in the life of tribal people.
2. Make a list of holy places that you know about. Why do places become holy?
3. Look up the following words in a dictionary and write down their meanings in your notebook: sanctuary, shrine and miracle.
4. Find some pictures of holy places and draw them in your notebook.

If you visited a holy place you might discover a wood carving, a stone figure or a picture which would be a symbol (*see* page 13) of the spirit or god. The spirits and gods are invisible but tribal people try to imagine what they look like. Tribal people are not really concerned with the symbol or representation as such but with what it stands for. The spirit or god is somehow present in the symbol or representation. That is why, for example, a statue of a god receives special attention. A holy man attached to the shrine is responsible for feeding and clothing the god.

Why do you think tribal people feel they need to make symbols of the spirits and gods they worship?

An Indian burial ground is also a sacred place. Why do you think this is?

5

Myths—Stories of the Gods

Myths are important stories which are found everywhere. They are stories about what the gods have done and what they continue to do for people. These myths explain and describe how the world and people were created, and how evil came into the world. Myths are not only about the beginnings of religion but about the whole life of people: their hunting; their skill in using wood or metal. In the myths the gods are responsible for giving people the gift of fire, the knowledge necessary to build houses and tame animals. Perhaps the most important gifts that the gods give to the people are the laws by which they live. How these came about are described in the myths.

Tell me a story

The Sun King

Perhaps you are familiar with some myths already from your study of Ancient Rome and Ancient Greece? For example the Greek myth that describes how Prometheus stole fire from the gods or the story of the god Apollo who rides his fiery chariot through the sky, which represents the movement of the sun (*see* page 6).

Then there are the Nordic myths – can you find out the significance of our naming the weekdays Wednesday and Thursday?

From Egyptian mythology we learn that the god Ra travels across the sky in his boat – once again representing the movement of the sun.

Do you know any other myths?

It is important to remember that these are not just simple stories but helped people to make sense of the world in which they lived. In the opening chapter of this book we said that people ask questions because they find themselves in a world full of mystery and wonder. In coming to terms with this mystery and trying to make sense of it, myths fulfil an important function.

Along with many others, tribal people have their myths – important stories of the gods and what they have done at important points in human life. Although these stories describe what the people believe happened way back at the beginning of time, they are told over and over again because they explain so many of the mysteries they have to face.

Who made the earth?

Where do human beings come from?

How did human beings first come to use fire?

The answers to these mysteries lie in the power of the gods they worship. These myths are told over and over again because they continue to be grateful for what the gods have done for them. The myths are taken seriously because they provide so many explanations for mysteries in the world around them. Myths are important to tribal people throughout their lives.

If the sun is pictured as a human being he might become a glorious king travelling across the sky in a golden chariot. The wind in the trees might be thought of as the voice of a beautiful goddess. Nature is full of sound and movement and appears to be very much alive. What gives it life? All of a sudden it can be full of powerful figures who cause the sound and movement.

Tribal people see the world as full of powers which are responsible for all that happens. These powers are the gods and goddesses who are given names and are imagined to be like human beings. They are the chief characters in the myths.

It is very difficult to know when the first myths were told, as most of them were passed on from generation to generation by word of mouth. For tribal people, their myths originated with the gods themselves and were revealed to their ancestors.

A statue of the Roman goddess of hunting—Diana

Things to do

1. In your own words explain what the word 'myth' means. Write down your explanation in your notebook.
2. Why are myths very important in the lives of tribal people?
3. Find out what you can about some of the myths from Ancient Rome, Greece and Egypt. Retell them in your own words and possibly put them in play form.

It is now time to look at some of these myths for ourselves. As you will see these myths are taken from many different parts of the world.

Creation myths (or how the world began)

One myth comes from a North American Indian tribe called the Winnebago.

'In the beginning there was only the earthmaker and he began to think of what he should do. Feeling very confused he began to cry and the tears fell down from his face. After some time he looked below and saw something bright. The bright objects were his tears which had flowed together to become the seas.'

'Earthmaker began to think again. He thought "It seems that whatever I wish will happen, just as my tears have become the seas." So he wished for light and it became light. Then he wished for the earth and the earth appeared. Then the earthmaker decided to make someone like himself. So he took a piece of earth and made it like himself. Then the earthmaker tried to talk to what he had made but it did not answer. He saw that what he had made had no brain or tongue. So the earthmaker gave a brain and tongue to what he had made and it nearly said something but it was not very clear. So the earthmaker breathed into its mouth and talked to it again. This time it answered.'

Things to do

1. In the myth, how did the earthmaker create sea, light and earth?
2. Why do you think the Winnebago Indians believe that the sea is made of tears?
3. Why do you think the Winnebago believed that human beings should be grateful to the earthmaker?

Another myth which also comes from North America is told by the Indians of Omaha.

'In the beginning all things were in the mind of Wakonda, the Great Spirit. All creatures, including men, were spirits. These spirits moved between heaven and earth. They were looking for a place where they could live in a bodily form. They tried to live on the sun and the moon but they found these places difficult to live on. They descended to the earth but they found it was covered in water and there was no dry land. They were very upset. Suddenly a great rock appeared from the water. The rock burst into flames and the water became steam which floated into the air to become clouds. Dry land appeared where grass and trees grew. The spirits descended and became flesh and blood. They lived very happily on earth and were grateful to Wakonda, the maker of all things.'

Things to do

1. According to this myth, human beings are made up of two parts. What are they?
2. How does this myth explain the creation of clouds?

Myths describing the origin of death

One of the greatest mysteries for people is how death came into the world. Here are three myths which explain this mystery. The first comes from Melanesia (*see also* page 20).

'In the beginning men and women never died. When they grew old they shed their skins like snakes. Then the men and women would be young again.'

'Once upon a time an old woman went to the stream to change her skin. She threw her old skin into the water and it began to float down the river. Then the woman, who was now young-looking, went home. Unfortunately, her child refused to recognise his changed mother and started to cry. The child knew that his mother was old and not like this young woman. To keep the child quiet she went back to the river and found her old skin and put it on. From that time on people stopped shedding their skins and died.'

This myth comes from Indonesia.

'In the beginning the sky was very near the earth and the Creator, who lived in the sky, let down his gifts to men at the end of a rope. One day the Creator let down a stone at the end of his rope. The first mother and father on the earth refused to take the stone and asked the Creator for something else. The Creator hauled up the stone and let the rope down again with a banana on the end. The first parents took the banana. Then a voice from heaven said, "Because you have chosen this, your life will be like the banana. When the banana tree gives its fruit the tree dies; so you shall die and your children also. If you had chosen the stone, your life would be like it, changeless and going on forever." The man and woman were very upset about their choice but it was too late. Through the eating of a banana death came into the world.'

Another myth comes from the Congo in Africa and is very similar to the last one.

'Once upon a time, long ago, the Supreme God offered the first men and women a choice of two packets. They had to choose one of them. The first packet contained beautiful pearls and jewels. The second packet contained immortality, the chance to live forever. The women were very worried about what they looked like and they wanted to be very beautiful. So the women grabbed the first packet and gave up the chance to have immortality.'

Things to do

1. In these last two myths who was responsible for bringing death into the world?
2. In these myths, how does death first come about?
3. Why do you think people die? What would happen if nobody died?

Myths concerned with the Sun

We have already seen that the forces in nature, like the sun, play an important part in the lives of tribal people. The sun provides heat and light which people need if they are to survive. This myth about the sun comes from Polynesia, and describes one of the events in the life of Maui, a great heavenly hero.

'One day Maui went to the far end of the world and acquired a magical jaw-bone which he made into a weapon. Maui decided he would make the day longer so that human beings would have more daylight to work in. So Maui hid by the gate through which the sun-god passed every morning. As the sun-god emerged out of the gate Maui attacked and injured him. The sun could then only move very slowly across the sky.'

Another myth is told by the Pygmies of Central Africa. The Pygmies are very anxious that the sun should shine each day after its disappearance during the night.

'As the sun dies in the evening the Supreme God, Knonvun, collects the broken pieces of the stars and puts them in his sack. Very early in the morning he tosses the pieces of stars at the sun so that it can rise as beautiful as ever.'

Things to do

1. How is this myth different from the others we have looked at? (Clue: how often does the sun shine?)

Myths describing how fire first came to men

Fire is very important to people as it gives warmth and people can cook over it. So it is not surprising that tribal people ask the question, 'Where did fire come from?' The first myth comes from tribal people who live in the region of the Upper Nile in Africa. The heavenly hero in this myth is a dog.

'In the beginning all the fire belonged to the sky gods. One day a dog ran towards where the fire was situated and burnt his tail. The dog howled in pain and threw himself into the bushes. Because the land in Africa is very dry, the grass soon caught fire and that is when human beings first came and gathered the flames for their own use.'

This myth comes from the Sudan also in Africa. These people live quite near to those of the Upper Nile. This myth tells of a rather mischievous god called Tule, who likes a bit of fun but who also brings many gifts to the people.

'One day Tule visited a blacksmith and, quite by accident, his cloak caught fire. Tule ran away in fear in the direction of the trees. He begged the fire to leave him and settle in the trees. The fire obeyed and settled in the trees. Since that time human beings have been able to produce fire by rubbing two sticks together because fire lives in the trees.'

Things to do

1. Why do you think these myths are very similar in places?
2. Ask your science teacher why it is possible to make a fire by rubbing two sticks together. Here we have an example of how science and myth are describing the same thing—how to make fire.

Myths that explain the origin of certain plants

Many tribal people use plants which they find round about them. These plants are very helpful in their lives and it is not surprising that they ask the question 'Where do such plants come from?'

The first myth comes from a North American Indian tribe called the Hitchti. The people of the Hitchti tribe use tobacco, particularly when they smoke their peace pipes. They believe that tobacco can bring peace.

'Once upon a time a man and a girl who were deeply in love went for a walk in the forest. After some time they kissed each other and then agreed to get married. Later, on a hunting trip, the man returned to the spot where he had kissed the girl and found a pretty flower with scented leaves. He took the plant back to his tribe and told them of his discovery. The people of the tribe said, "When it is dried, we will smoke it, and call it 'Where We came Together.' " The chiefs of the tribe claimed that because the man and woman were so at peace and happy when tobacco was made, it would be smoked at the times when peace was being made between the tribes.'

The next myth comes from the Chaco Indian tribe of South America. The Chaco Indians use a rare plant which is burnt and the ashes used as salt.

'It is told that the god Cotaa created a miraculous tree which gave food and drink to the hungry people. One day a mischievous spirit called Neepec tipped a jar filled with tears over the tree and spoilt the taste. When the god Cotaa returned and saw what was done, he turned the damage into good and explained that the salty taste might serve for making meat dishes more edible.'

Things to do

1. Write down two reasons why salt would be very valuable to tribal people.
2. What part of this story is similar to the first creation myth that you have read?
3. What character in this myth is not found in any of the others?

How the myths are used

The myths take very seriously all that
the gods have done for the people in the
past. They are told over and over again
to remind the people how thankful they
must be for what the gods have done.

These myths might be told each year
at particular festival times or during
worship. For example, the creation
myths might be told at each New Year
celebration to ensure that the god's
creative power remains with the tribe for
the coming year as it was at the
beginning of time. The myth about the
tobacco plant might be told as the
tobacco seed is planted so as to ensure a
good crop.

From this we can see that a myth is
used in the present and it also links the
people to important events in the past.

Things to do

1. At what times do you think the
   myths about the sun and fire might
   be used by tribal people?
2. Many of the myths are not merely
   spoken but are often acted out. The
   holy man of the tribe might take the
   part of the god. Select one of the
   myths you have read and make it into
   a play. When you have finished
   writing the play try to act it out.
3. Make a drawing of one of the myths
   you have read.

6

Festivals and Ceremonies

People, everywhere, look forward to festivals and ceremonies of one sort or another. Excitement mounts as preparations are made, because festivals are occasions for fun and usually involve family and friends. Festivals occur at special times of the year and that usually means a holiday from our usual work.

One such festival that we celebrate in Britain is Christmas. Apart from giving presents, sending cards, and eating too much we are reminded of the birth of Jesus Christ some 2000 years ago. At Christmas, Christians in schools, churches and at home remember the birth of Jesus by singing carols and

Do you recognise this picture? What are the children doing?

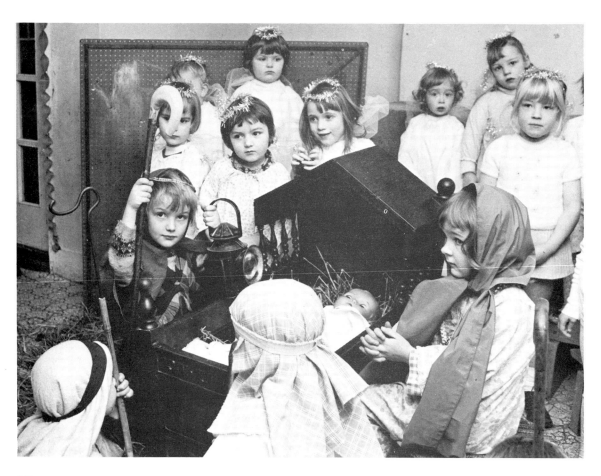

reminding themselves of the story of Jesus' birth. Some people even act out the story of the birth in the form of a nativity play. Perhaps you can remember taking part in a nativity play at school. Why do you think people remember the birth of Jesus Christ?

What we do and say when celebrating Christmas is known as the 'ritual' of Christmas. Singing carols, reading and acting out the stories are examples of the rituals connected with Christmas. People want to involve themselves in the 'spirit of Christmas.' What do you think this means?

Christmas is a religious festival, but there are others which we celebrate that are connected with the changing seasons. Can you think of any such festivals?

A harvest festival scene. Why do we celebrate harvest festivals?

Things to do

1. Make a list of the festivals we celebrate in this country. Write down the name of the festival, what we do to celebrate it and why we do so. Follow the example given below.

Festival	How we celebrate it	Why we celebrate it
Christmas	Carols, nativity plays, presents, turkey	To remind ourselves of the birth of Jesus Christ

2. Look up the following words in a dictionary and write down their meanings in your notebook: festival and ritual.

3. Draw a picture to show how we celebrate one of the festivals listed in question one.

Tribal people, too, enjoy their festivals and look forward to them as much as we do. They are occasions of joy and celebration. The members of the tribe remember what the gods and spirits have done for them at all the important stages in the life of the tribe. By remembering the gods and spirits at special times, the tribe continue to show their dependence on the gods and spirits they worship. Each year the tribe has to face hardships and difficulties. Each year the power of evil tries to upset the smooth running of the tribe. How can the tribe overcome the power of evil? This can only be done if the gods and spirits are honoured and remembered. Tribal people believe that the power of the gods and spirits that helped them in the past will help them in the future. At the New Year festival the people call upon the power of the gods and spirits to shake off the evil of the previous year and prepare the way for the new one so that the tribe can make a fresh start. At harvest time the tribe offers the first crop of food to the gods as a sign of gratitude, and they hope that the gods will continue to look after them.

A harvest offering in the Nicobar Islands (South East Asia). It is made up of fruit and vegetables

Aborigines taking part in the Moon Legend Dance

Festivals involving the whole tribe

The majority of these festivals are connected with the changing seasons and the forces in nature like the sun, moon and rain which are responsible for these changes. Therefore, festivals celebrating the New Year, Spring and harvest are common among tribal people. The changing seasons and what they bring are controlled by the gods and spirits. They have the power to decide the fortunes of the tribe during the year. At each festival the power of the gods and spirits are celebrated to ensure the survival of the tribe. We shall now take a look at some of these festivals.

The 'Iroquois' Indians of America have six regular festivals connected with the growth of the food they eat. During the first festival of the year the people of the tribe 'purify' themselves by 'confessing' all that they have done wrong in the past year. In olden times the people would swallow sticks to make themselves sick. By being sick they were showing the spirits that all the evil had gone out of them. The other festivals are connected with the planting of corn, collecting the first strawberries, the appearance of the first ears of corn and the harvest celebration. Finally the Iroquois thank the Great Power for all he has done.

New Year's Day celebrations in Nigeria

At the New Year festival of the 'Ijaw' people in Africa, palm leaves are cut from the trees. The people beat each other with the leaves. They are shaking off all the evils of the previous year. Then they throw the leaves into the river and watch them float away. When this is done they are ready to face the new year.

The Aborigines of Australia suffer frequently from long periods of drought and so one of their most important festivals is connected with rain-making. This festival is performed by the chief 'Kunki' (or 'medicine man') and his assistants with the help of the rest of the people. To bring rain they have to persuade the 'Mura Muras' (or 'rain-making spirits') to send it. The festival begins with the whole tribe digging a hole in the ground and building a hut over it. The old men of the tribe take their places inside the hut and the Kunki cuts their arms with a sharp piece of flint. The blood from their wounds is showered over the rest of the tribe who sit around the hut. Two assistants of the Kunki, also with their arms cut, throw handfuls of feathers into the air. The blood represents the rain and the feathers represent clouds. At the end of the festival the men break down the hut with their heads. This represents the breaking of the clouds and when it falls down this signifies the downpour of rain. During the ceremony prayers for rain are said to the Mura Muras. If no rain comes the people believe the spirits are angry.

Things to do

1. Look up the following words in a dictionary and write down their meanings in your notebook: purify and confess.
2. In this country we make New Year resolutions. What is a resolution? What resolutions do you think the Ijaw people of Africa make as they watch the leaves float down the river?
3. The Aborigines act out their rain-making ceremony. Write a short play based on this ceremony.

An Aborigine pounding rock as part of the rain making ceremony

Tribal festivals are very lively

What happens at the festivals

As you might imagine the festivals of tribal people are lively occasions. The people dance and sing just as we do when we celebrate a special occasion. The tribe usually follows a rigid pattern of ritual (*see* page 79) which includes prayer and possibly a sacrifice. The festivals are times for fun but the people must not forget that their main concern is to renew their contact with the spirits and gods. The ritual must be strictly followed because it has been revealed to them by the gods and spirits. If something is done or said that is wrong then the spirits and gods will be offended.

At festival times the people are reminded of what the spirits and gods have done by the re-telling of their myths. Myths are important because they show how the power of the gods and spirits was responsible for creating and maintaining the life of the tribe. Through the re-telling of myths this same power will continue to help the tribe. The people of the tribe might act out the myth to make the festival more exciting and meaningful. For example, the people of the tribe might act out the myth of creation during a New Year festival. This would ensure that the power that was present in the creation of life would be present in the forthcoming year.

The acting out of the myth and the other rituals connected with the festival might appear meaningless to the present members of the tribe. However, they are justified by the words, 'The Fathers or Ancestors taught us to do these things'. Like the myths, the rituals connected with the festivals have been handed down from generation to generation. It was the fathers or the ancestors who learnt the myths and rituals from the gods themselves.

Celebrating the festival of Ogun, the god of iron, amongst the Yoruba of Nigeria (*see* pages 33 and 37)

Ceremonies concerning the individual

It is often said that the majority of people in this country only enter a church on three occasions in their lives, to be christened, married and buried. Many people go to church more regularly than this but it shows that these important events in the life of an individual are still connected with religion.

Life journey

What stages of life are represented in this picture?

Where religion plays an important part in the lives of the people, the key moments of birth, coming of age, marriage and death are deeply religious occasions when religious rituals (*see* page 79) are performed. Although these occasions involve family and friends, the main concern is with the individual who is actually moving from one important stage of life to another.

A person is born, reaches adulthood or 'comes of age', marries and dies. Life can be pictured as a long journey and a person changes at certain stages on this journey and steps out on a new phase of his or her life. Each change is accompanied by some sort of festival or ceremony to show that this change has taken place. We call the ceremonies that mark these changes in life 'rituals (or 'rites') of passage'. Can you suggest why they are called this?

Things to do

1. What sorts of things take place, in this country, at each of the following stages in the life of a person: birth, coming of age, marriage, death?
2. What part does religion still play at any of these stages?
3. How do you think that these 'rituals of passage' differ from the festivals and ceremonies involving the whole tribe that we looked at in the last section?
4. Have you ever attended a christening, a marriage or a funeral? Write down what you can remember about such an occasion.
5. In your books draw a straight line and write on it the important stages in life. Can you think of any others that have not been mentioned?

We have seen that tribal people around the world believe that health and prosperity depend on the good will of the gods and spirits they worship. As people grow up and change from one stage of life to another the help of the gods and spirits is particularly sought after. Why do you think this is? We shall now look at some of these 'ritual passages' from various parts of the world.

Birth

Among tribal people pregnancy and birth are surrounded by many special rituals and ceremonies that are performed to prevent evil harming the mother and child. It must be remembered that many tribal people might not have the medical and hospital care that we have to make the birth a success, so prayers and sacrifices are offered to the gods and spirits to ask for their help.

Among the Tzotzil people of Mexico, a pregnant woman must avoid seeing dead bodies and must not make fun of deformed people, or her own child may become a dwarf, a hunchback or a stutterer. As soon as a Tzotzil woman becomes pregnant, prayers are said to the earth, and to the ancestors to ensure a safe delivery. After the birth the umbilical cord is taken by the father. If the child is a boy, he ties the cord to a high branch of a tree and prays that the lad will be able to climb without fear. If it is a girl he puts the cord by the hearth to show that she will help her mother and, later, become a good wife herself.

The naming of the child is another important ceremony connected with birth. Among the Yoruba people of Nigeria a child is given the name of either Babatunde ('Father has returned') or Yetunde ('Mother has returned') if it is born shortly after the death of a grandparent of the same sex. The grandfather or grandmother has been reborn.

Things to do

1. Why do you think that in many tribal societies the pregnant mother is kept away from normal village life?
2. What's in a name? The Yoruba child who is born shortly after the death of a grandparent is given a special name. Even the names we give children mean something. Do you know what your name means? If you don't, try to find out.
3. The idea that someone is reborn into another life on earth is called 're-incarnation'. Find out as much as you can about re-incarnation'.

Coming of age

'Coming of age' is the time when young people are recognised as adults and no longer children. The idea of joining the adult world is sometimes known as 'initiation' into this new stage of life. Among tribal people it is normally the boys who undergo an initiation ceremony into adulthood but in some countries the girls, too, take part in a special ritual to show that they have now grown up. From the time of his initiation the boy takes his place as an adult member of the tribe and he is taught the religious customs and myths of the tribe. This knowledge is thought to be secret for if it is revealed to outsiders it could be used to work harmful magic on the tribe. It is quite frequent for the boy to undergo a test of strength and endurance to prove he is worthy of being called a man.

In one Australian Aborigine tribe, the boy shows his readiness for manhood by undergoing an extremely painful operation during which one of his front teeth is knocked out. By not crying out the boy proves he is ready to face the hardships of adult life. The removal of a tooth also represents the death of boyhood and the return to life as an adult. This is accomplished by the work of a spirit and manhood is marked by the giving of a new name.

An Aborigine boy having a tooth knocked out as part of an initiation ceremony

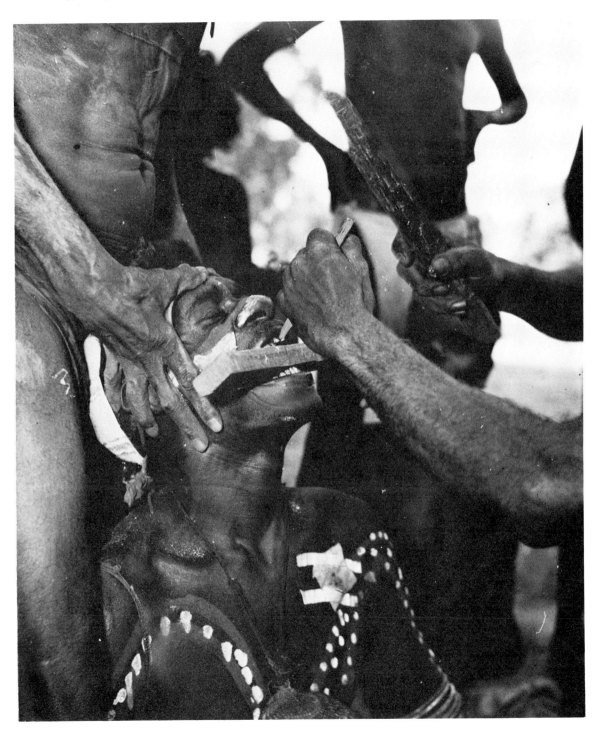

A marriage festival in Africa

Marriage

In this country many people tend to think of marriage as really only involving the bride and groom. For other people, including tribal people, the family has a much more important part to play in the arrangements and performance of the ceremony. With marriage comes the breaking away from one family group to join with another. Normally it is the bride who joins the groom's family. Even in this country this is shown by the bride taking the name of her husband. In Africa the bridegroom's family would make a gift to the family of the bride as compensation for their loss.

The marriage ceremony itself shows the breaking of family ties. Among the Yoruba of Nigeria you might be surprised to find the bride in tears as she is taken by force from her family. You will quickly learn that the bride is merely pretending to be sad because, after all, she is leaving her family. She is expected to show feelings of sadness because an expression of joy at such a time would be out of place. At all stages the spirits of the dead ancestors are consulted to ensure that the marriage will be a success.

Two Indian girls prepare for marriage

For the Kol people of Bengal in India marriage not only means joining a new group but the gaining of a soul. Power and prosperity comes from the spirits of two trees, the mango and the mahua. (*Look back to* page 28 on Totem Spirits.) At first the bridegroom marries the mango and the bride the mahua by embracing the trees. The couple have now acquired their souls and the marriage can continue. As you may gather, the couple do not actually marry the trees but why do you think they go through the ceremony of embracing them?

A Toraja funeral Festival. The bamboo pavilion is burnt and it will be rebuilt in the spirit world and await the coming of the dead ancestor.

Death

For many, the death of a person is an unhappy time not only because they may be losing someone who has been close to them but also because they may be unsure of what comes after death (*see* pages 11 and 12). This uncertainty can often cause fear. Tribal people, too, are frightened of the dead because the power of the dead spirit can bring bad luck (*look back* to pages 25-27). For this reason the dead are buried with great care; a word or action out of place during the ceremony could result in the dead person bringing bad luck. The dead depend on the living to perform the death ceremony correctly so that they may rest peacefully. The living depend on the dead to link the family with the spiritual power which the ancestors possess. When the ceremony is performed correctly both the living and the dead are much happier.

If you were to visit a funeral ceremony of the Toraja people of Indonesia, you might think you have come upon a carnival rather than a funeral. The people who gather for the funeral are in very high spirits and they appear far from sad. Processions of people arrive at the funeral field with buffalo ready to be sacrificed in honour of the dead person. A large pavilion is built from bamboo and everyone awaits the procession which brings the body to the funeral. The dead must be given a good send off. The dead person is about to become an ancestor. The coffin containing the dead person is brought onto the field. In a special ceremony the bamboo pavilion is

Wooden statues of Toraja ancestors

burnt and buffalo are sacrificed. The Torajas believe that the pavilion and the buffalo will go ahead of the dead spirit and be there in the spirit world to await its arrival. The body is taken to the grave site where it is to be buried. A wooden statue is made and placed in a sacred place alongside other statues. The ceremony is complete and the dead person takes its place among the ancestors.

Things to do

1. Why do you think the Toraja people are not sad at one of their funerals?
2. With the information you have been given, write a story about what happens at a Toraja funeral. Illustrate your story with a picture.

Index